はじめての
TOEIC BRIDGE®
L & R テスト
完全模試 3回分

鈴木 瑛子　渡邉 淳

ask

●英文作成 .... Daniel Warriner

●イラスト .... 杠聡

●音声収録・編集 ...... 合同会社ユニバ

●ナレーター .... Rachel Walzer　Emma Howard

　　　　　　　　　　　 Iain Gibb　Stuart O

はじめに

　TOEIC Bridge テストは、2019 年 6 月に新形式となり、TOEIC テストと同じように、聞く・読む・話す・書くの英語 4 技能を測定するテストになりました。

　本書は『受けてみよう！ TOEIC BRIDGE テスト模試 3 回分』を全面改訂し、TOEIC Bridge Listening & Reading テストの新形式に合わせた問題を作成し、解答解説を加えたものです。

　ここでは本書を使った学習に取り組む際に気を付けていただきたいことをお伝えします。

◆本番と同じ環境で解く！

　本書の模試に初めて取り組む時には、ぜひ、1 時間、問題を解くことだけに集中できる環境を整えてください。できる限り、本番に近い環境を用意しましょう。練習でやっていることが本番で出ます。本気で取り組むことで、英語力はもちろん、集中力など本当の実力がわかります。

◆1 つの模試を 3 回解く！

　たくさん問題を解くことで、試験に慣れることができます。本書では第 1 ～ 3 回のテストにそれぞれ 3 回ずつ、計 9 回挑戦するようおすすめしています。効果的な挑戦方法は「本書の使い方」(p.6-8) を見てください。試験内容や形式に沿った英語の基礎知識を身につけることで、効率的なスコアアップにつながります。

◆答え合わせのあとが大事！

　時間を測って模試を解いたあと、そこからが英語の実力をつける絶好の機会です。本書「徹底復習トレーニング」(p.9-11) に、各パートごとにスコアアップに効果的なトレーニング方法を載せました。これらは TOEIC Bridge L&R テストだけでなく、そのまま TOEIC L&R テストの勉強にも応用できるトレーニング方法です。

　TOEIC Bridge L&R テストを通し、さまざまな場面で使える英語力を伸ばすためのお手伝いができれば幸いです。

　最後になりましたが、本書の企画段階から出版に至るまでご尽力いただいたアスク出版の川田直樹氏に心から感謝申し上げます。

鈴木瑛子　渡邉淳

目次

第1回テスト

第2回テスト

第3回テスト

別冊　解答・解説

本書の使い方

　本書は「とにかく問題をたくさん解きたい」という人のために完全模試3回分を収録しています。多くの問題に挑戦することで、出題傾向を把握したり、時間配分をマスターしたりしましょう。また、問題の英文を素材にして、トレーニングを行うことで、大きな実力アップが期待できます。

❖ TOEIC Bridge L&R テストを知る！

　このテストを初めて受験する方や、問題形式をよく知らない方は「TOEIC Bridge L&R テストとは？」(p.12 〜 16) からスタートしましょう。テストの主旨や問題形式を理解することで、問題に挑戦しやすくなります。

　もし問題形式などの基本的な情報をすでに知っている人は、それらのページは読み飛ばして、早速、第1回テスト（TEST1）に挑戦しましょう。

❖効果的な模試の使い方を知る！

　本番のテストの問題には、本書で取り上げた問題と似たような問題が出題される可能性があります。その際に、確実に正解できるように、模試を使い倒すことをオススメします。

［挑戦1回目］

① テストを受験・採点する

　リスニングは音声の指示に従って、解答を進めます。約25分間です。その後すぐに、リーディングに取り掛かり、制限時間35分を厳守しましょう。もし制限時間内に終わらなければ、残りの問題は正解数にはカウントしないものの、自力で解きましょう。

② 間違った問題の解説を読み、理解する

　解説で理解できない部分があれば、他の参考書やインターネットで調べ尽くしてください。理解できないままだと、似た問題で間違ってしまうことになります。ここで手を抜かないようにしてください。

③ 別冊解答・解説の扉ページにある「チェックシート」に記入する

　間違った問題を記録しておくことで、自分が間違う傾向も把握できるため、対

策がしやすくなります。また、間違った問題だけを解き直すことができて、復習の効率が上がります。

チェックシート　☞

別冊第1〜3回それぞれの扉にあります。

No.	正解	チェック		No.	正解	チェック
1	B	☑☐☐		26	C	☐☐
2	C	☐☐☐		27	D	☐☐
3	D	☐☐☐		28	B	☐☐

④ 全問題でトレーニング（詳しくは p.9 〜 11）を行う

　解説を理解しただけでは、英語力はほとんど上がりません。解説を理解した後の復習によって、英語力を上げていきましょう。トレーニングには時間はかかりますが、やればやっただけ、スコアアップという形で跳ね返ってきます。

［挑戦2回目］
① 1回目から約1週間後に、同じテストを受験・採点する

② 間違った問題の解説を読み、理解する

③ 別冊解答・解説の扉ページにある「チェックシート」に記入する

　連続して間違った問題がひと目でわかります。その問題は弱点である可能性が高いため、解説にある「出題パターン」もおさえておきましょう。

出題パターンマーク　☞

問題には出題パターンが示されています。

付加疑問文

語彙問題　動詞

④ 間違った問題のみトレーニングを行う

　連続して間違った問題はもちろん、新たに間違った問題もトレーニングを行いましょう。何かしらの理由でミスをしているため、トレーニングを重ねることで、ミスが減っていきます。気を抜かずにいきましょう。

［挑戦 3 回目］

① 2 回目の挑戦から約 1 週間後に、同じテストを受験・採点する

　3 回目では、全問正解を目指します。難易度の高い問題も、トレーニングができていれば、正解できるはずです。

② 間違った問題の解説を読み、理解する

③ 別冊解答・解説の扉ページにある「チェックシート」に記入する

④ 間違った問題のみトレーニングを行う

❖音声ダウンロード

本書ではデジタルオーディオプレーヤーでご利用いただける音声データのダウンロードを行なっています。

★ブラウザからダウンロードする

　ウェブブラウザを使って、以下のサイトにアクセスしてください。

『はじめての TOEIC BRIDGE® L&R テスト　完全模試 3 回分』

アスクブックス　ウェブサイト

https://www.ask-books.com/978-4-86639-396-4

★アプリにダウンロードする

　abceed（エービーシード）　株式会社 Globee が提供するサービスです。

---

https://www.abceed.com/

　アプリで、本書の書名を検索してダウンロードしてください。

徹底復習トレーニング

　模試などの問題演習には復習がつきものです。「復習する」と言っても、具体的に何をすればよいかがわからない方のために、具体的な学習内容を用意しました。参考にしてください。

　復習には時間がかかりますが、このトレーニングをどれだけやり込めるかで、成長の度合いは変わってきます。しっかりやり切りましょう！

LISTENING TEST

PART 1（画像選択問題）

★ディクテーションをする

トレーニング方法：

　英語を聞いて、書き取る。途中で止めずに、もう一度聞きたかったら、最初から何度も聞く。

理由：

　短い英語を聞き取って、画像と照らし合わせるためには、その英語を一瞬記憶する必要があります。このトレーニングを通して、英語を自分の頭に残す機会を増やしましょう。

PART 2（応答問題）

★リッスンアンドリピートをする

トレーニング方法：

　英語を聞いて、その内容を声に出す。聞いたら止めて、声に出す流れ。ディクテーション同様、もう一度聞くならば、最初から聞くほうが望ましい。

理由：

PART 1 同様、短い英語を記憶する必要があるため、一度聞いて記憶する練習をしましょう。少し負荷が高いですが、トレーニングでここまでやっておけば、問題を解くのは楽になります。

PART 3（会話問題）
PART 4（説明文問題）

> ★ ❶ 英語を理解する
> ★ ❷ 英語を見ながら、何度も聞く

トレーニング方法：

流れてくる英語を理解する。日本語訳を参考にしながら、単語や文法の不明点をなくす。理解度を 100 パーセントにした素材を何度も聞く。

理由：

理解できていないものを何度聞いても、英語力は上がらないからです。理解することに時間をかけましょう。それが終わった後で、まとまった英語を聞くことに慣れていきましょう。

READING TEST

PART 1（短文穴埋め問題）
PART 2（長文穴埋め問題）

> ★セルフ解説をする

トレーニング方法：

正解の選択肢を選んだ理由を説明する。「直感」や「なんとなく」という言葉は封印する。

理由：

　同じ／似ている問題を間違う理由の一つとして、今まで解いた問題への理解が中途半端な可能性があります。そのため、「なぜ正解がこれなのか」という、正解へのプロセスを説明することで、理解度が明らかになります。セルフ解説が詰まってしまうところは、自分の弱点である可能性が高いため、解説を再読することをオススメします。

PART 3（読解問題）

> **★ ❶ 英語を理解する**
> **★ ❷ 英語を読む**

トレーニング方法：

　書かれている英語を理解する。日本語訳を参考にしながら、単語や文法の不明点をなくす。理解度を 100 パーセントにした素材を何度も読む。

理由：

　LISTENING の PART 3, 4 と同様、長文パートとはじっくり向き合うことで、英語力が伸びていきます。単語や文法の不明点をなくすことで知識が増えて、読める英語が増えていきます。

TOEIC Bridge L&Rテストとは？

　TOEIC Bridge Listening & Reading Tests は、英語学習初級者から中級者を対象とした、日常生活で活きる"英語で聞く・読む能力"を測定するテストです。

　TOEIC Bridge の「Bridge」は、「橋」という意味です。つまり、このテスト名には「TOEIC への架け橋」になるように、との思いが込められています。

　TOEIC Bridge テストは TOEIC に進む前段階で取り組めるテストとして開発され、2001 年にスタートしました。その後、「聞く・読む」能力に「話す・書く」能力を加えた 4 技能を測定できる新形式のテスト（TOEIC Bridge L&R テストと TOEIC Bridge S&W テスト）が開発され、公開テストでは 2019 年 6 月から開始、また団体特別受験制度（IP:Institutional Program）では 2020 年 4 月から導入されています。

　TOEIC テストでは日常生活やグローバルビジネスでの場面を想定した幅広い内容を扱っているのに対し、TOEIC Bridge テストは英語初・中級者に合わせ、より身近な日常生活を題材に基礎的な英語力を測定します。

　TOEIC L&R テストと比べ、TOEIC Bridge L&R テストは難易度がやさしいという以外に、次のような特徴があります。

　　1. 日常的で身近な題材が中心
　　2. 問題数と受験時間が半分（100 問／ 1 時間）
　　3. リスニングスピードはゆっくり

　日常生活に関わる英語中心、問題数と受験時間も半分、リスニングスピードもゆっくりということで学生や英語初・中級者が取り組みやすくなっています。

　英語の学習は根気がいるものです。目標を持たずに学習を進めても、なかなか長続きしません。英語初・中級者にとって、TOEIC Bridge L&R テストの受験は、モチベーションを高める、よい目標となると思います。

❖ TOEIC Bridge L&R テストと TOEIC L&R テスト の違いは？

　TOEIC L&R テストと TOEIC Bridge L&R テストを比べ、どちらが自分にあっているのか悩んでいる人もいるでしょう。TOEIC L&R テストは難しいなあと感じる方や英語学習初期段階の方には TOEIC Bridge の受験をおすすめします。以下の比較表も参考にして、自分にはどちらが合っているのか判断してみてください。（※ 2023 年 10 月現在 / 受験料など変更される可能性があります。）

	TOEIC Bridge L&R テスト	TOEIC L&R テスト
測定する能力	初・中級者の「聞く」「読む」英語力	「聞く」「読む」英語力
出題範囲	日常生活	ビジネス・日常生活
テストの形式と構成	約 1 時間のテスト リスニング約 25 分間 リーディング 35 分間	約 2 時間のテスト リスニング約 45 分間 リーディング 75 分間
問題数	100 問（リスニング 50 問 リーディング 50 問）	200 問（リスニング 100 問 リーディング 100 問）
解答方法	マークシート方式	マークシート方式
テスト結果	30 ～ 100 点（リスニング 15 ～ 50 点 リーディング 15 ～ 50 点）1 点刻みのスコアで評価	10 ～ 990 点（リスニング 5 ～ 495 点 リーディング 5 ～ 495 点）5 点刻みのスコアで評価
受験料	4,950 円（税込）	7,810 円（税込）

❖ テストの構成は？

　テスト構成は下表のように、まずリスニング・テストとリーディング・テストに分かれ、リスニングの中に PART 1 ～ 4、リーディングに PART 1 ～ 3 があり、計 7 つのパートで構成されています。

	リスニング				リーディング		
	PART 1	PART 2	PART 3	PART 4	PART 1	PART 2	PART 3
問題数	6 問	20 問	10 問	14 問	15 問	15 問	20 問
問題形式	4 択	4 択	4 択	4 択	4 択	4 択	4 択
試験時間	約 25 分間				35 分間		

［リスニング・テスト］

PART 1：Four Pictures ― 画像選択問題（6 問）

句や文を聞いて、4 つの絵の中から、その句や文を最もよく表す絵を選ぶ問題です。問題用紙には絵だけが提示されていて、読まれる音声は一度きりです。

PART 2：Question-Response ― 応答問題（20 問）

質問や発言を聞いて、4 つの選択肢の中から、応答として最も適切なものを選ぶ問題です。問題用紙には記載されていない英文の短い問いかけの音声が流れ、続いて記載されている (A) ～ (D) の 4 つの応答が読み上げられます。音声が読まれるのは一度きりです。

PART 3：Conversations ― 会話問題（10 問）

2 人の人物による短い会話を聞き、会話に関する 2 つの設問に解答する問題です。後半の 2 題には、看板やお知らせなどの簡単な補足図表を参照する問題もあります。ここでも音声が読まれるのは一度だけです。設問は 4 択形式です。

PART 4：Talks ― 説明文問題（14 問）

1 人の話し手による短いメッセージやお知らせなどを聞き、その内容に関する 2 つの設問に解答する問題です。後半の 2 題には、看板やお知らせなどの簡単な補足図表を参照する問題もあります。ここでも音声が読まれるのは一度だけです。

設問は 4 択形式です。

［リーディング・テスト］

PART 1：Sentence Completion — 短文穴埋め問題（15 問）

語や句が 1 カ所抜けている文を読み、それを完成させるのに最も適切な選択肢を選ぶ問題です。問題用紙に、空所を含んだ英文と (A) 〜 (D) の選択肢が提示されています。4 つの選択肢のなかから、空所を埋めるものを選び、意味の通る完全な文にします。

PART 2：Text Completion — 長文穴埋め問題（15 問）

語や句または文が 3 カ所抜けている文章を読み、それを完成させるのに最も適切な選択肢を選ぶ問題です。問題用紙に、空所を含んだ英文と (A) 〜 (D) の選択肢が提示されています。4 つの選択肢のなかから、空所を埋めるものを選び、意味の通る完全な文にします。

PART 3：Reading Comprehension — 読解問題（20 問）

1 つの文書を読んで、それに関する 2 つか 3 つの設問に解答する問題です。E メール・広告・お知らせ・ウェブページ・テキストメッセージなど、さまざまな英文を読み、その内容に関する設問に答えます。英文は 8 題出題され、それぞれに 2 〜 3 問の設問がついています。設問は 4 択形式。

❖成績はどのように算出される？

　TOEIC Bridge L&R テストの成績は、リスニング 15 〜 50 点、リーディング 15 〜 50 点、計 30 〜 100 点のスコアで評価されます（1 点刻み）。ここが、英検などの合格・不合格で成績を判定するテストとの大きな違いです。

　また、30 〜 100 点のスコアのほかに、「アビリティーズ・メジャード」と呼ばれる項目別正答率も算出されます。リスニングでは「適切な応答」「短い対話や会話」「短いトーク」「要点や述べられた事実の理解」、リーディングでは「語彙」「文法」「要点や述べられた事実の理解」「情報を伝える短い文書」の各 4 つの指標があり、自分の得意分野や弱点を知ることができます。

　ちなみに TOEIC Bridge L&R テストのスコアは単純に「1 問の配点×正解数」で算出されるわけではありません。受験回によってスコアのブレが生じないように統計処理を加えて算出されています。そのためスコアが 30 〜 100 点という値になっているのです。本書の模試を採点する際は便宜的に 1 問 1 点として計算してください。

TOEIC Bridge Listening & Reading Tests は、アメリカの非営利テスト開発機関 Educational Testing Service (ETS) により制作されています。ETS は TOEIC テストや TOEFL をはじめ、各種資格試験や国家試験を開発・制作・実施している世界最大規模の教育研究機関です。日本での実施・運営は、TOEIC テスト同様、一般財団法人 国際ビジネスコミュニケーション協会 (IIBC) によって行なわれており、問い合わせ窓口ともなっています。

IIBC の公式 Web サイトには、スケジュールや受験地、これまでの受験者数や平均スコアなど役立つ情報が多数、掲載されています。受験申込もこのサイトから行なうことができます。ぜひ一度アクセスしてみてください。

> **IIBC 公式サイト**
>
> https://www.iibc-global.org

［問い合わせ先］

一般財団法人 国際ビジネスコミュニケーション協会

◆ IIBC 試験運営センター
〒100-0014　東京都千代田区永田町 2-14-2　山王グランドビル
TEL: 03-5521-6033

◆名古屋事務所
TEL: 052-220-0286

◆大阪事務所
TEL: 06-6258-0224

受付時間はいずれも 10:00 ～ 17:00（土・日・祝日・年末年始を除く）
※受付時間については変更になる場合があるため公式サイトでご確認ください。

第 1 回テスト

TEST 1

解答・解説は

・・・・・・・・・・・・・・・・・・ 別冊 4 - 71 ページ

▶ 音声ファイル

トラック名

PART 1: T1_P1_Dir ▶ T1_P1_Q6
PART 2: T1_P2_Dir ▶ T1_P2_Q26
PART 3: T1_P3_Dir ▶ T1_P3_Q35-36
PART 4: T1_P4_Dir ▶ T1_P4_Q49-50

LISTENING

This is the Listening test. There are four parts to this test.

LISTENING PART 1

Directions: You will see a set of four pictures in your test book, and you will hear one short phrase or sentence. Look at the set of pictures. Choose the picture that the phrase or sentence best describes. Then mark the letter (A), (B), (C), or (D) on your answer sheet.

Look at the sample pictures below and listen to the phrase.

Example

You will hear: A man wearing headphones.

(A)

(B)

(C)

(D)
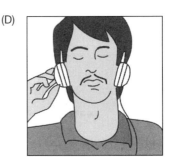

The best answer is (D), so you should mark the letter (D) on your answer sheet.

1. (A)

(B)

(C)

(D)

2. (A)

(B)

(C)

(D)

GO ON TO THE NEXT PAGE

3. (A) 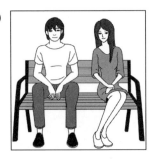 (B)

(C)  (D)

4. (A)  (B)

(C)  (D)

5. (A)

(B)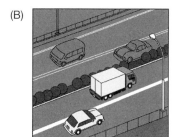

(C)

(D)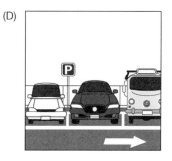

6. (A)

(B)

(C)

(D)

GO ON TO THE NEXT PAGE

LISTENING PART 2

Directions: You will hear some questions or statements. After each question or statement, you will hear and read four responses. Choose the best response to each question or statement. Then mark the letter (A), (B), (C), or (D) on your answer sheet.

Now listen to a sample question.

Example

You will hear:　　　　　　What time is it?

You will hear and read　　　(A) It's three o'clock.

　　　　　　　　　　　　(B) Several times.

　　　　　　　　　　　　(C) Near the hotel.

　　　　　　　　　　　　(D) Yes, it is.

The best answer is (A), so you should mark the letter (A) on your answer sheet.

---

7. Mark your answer on your answer sheet.

(A) Yes, it is.
(B) Silver and blue.
(C) In the parking lot.
(D) Well, I can drive.

8. Mark your answer on your answer sheet.

(A) Two or three pages.
(B) Mr. Reilly's classroom.
(C) The day after tomorrow.
(D) Yes, the payment is due.

9. Mark your answer on your answer sheet.

(A) A few months ago.
(B) At a furniture store.
(C) All right, I'll move them.
(D) For office supplies.

10. Mark your answer on your answer sheet.

    (A) No, an afternoon flight.
    (B) Traffic is terrible.
    (C) I left it on the train.
    (D) Yes, it does.

11. Mark your answer on your answer sheet.

    (A) For some renovations.
    (B) At 11 o'clock.
    (C) Probably in February.
    (D) Next to the bank.

12. Mark your answer on your answer sheet.

    (A) I couldn't find them.
    (B) It took a while.
    (C) Around your office.
    (D) Sure, I'll go this morning.

13. Mark your answer on your answer sheet.

    (A) The door is open.
    (B) Both are fine with me.
    (C) Actually, it's on that shelf.
    (D) The first topic.

14. Mark your answer on your answer sheet.

    (A) Ms. Dixon is.
    (B) It's down the hall.
    (C) Yes, that's right.
    (D) Stacking chairs.

15. Mark your answer on your answer sheet.

    (A) I'd like that very much.
    (B) No, not yet.
    (C) At the beginning.
    (D) It arrived there yesterday.

GO ON TO THE NEXT PAGE

16. Mark your answer on your answer sheet.

    (A) It's a lovely place.
    (B) I left them on your desk.
    (C) By bus is the easiest way.
    (D) How about right now?

17. Mark your answer on your answer sheet.

    (A) About five kilometers.
    (B) The last one starts soon.
    (C) Check the storage room.
    (D) Two more stops.

18. Mark your answer on your answer sheet.

    (A) Anytime next week.
    (B) Print out a few.
    (C) Shall we go somewhere else?
    (D) Which do you recommend?

19. Mark your answer on your answer sheet.

    (A) No, they didn't.
    (B) Oh, I'll wash them.
    (C) Some larger plates.
    (D) It usually does.

20. Mark your answer on your answer sheet.

    (A) At the stadium.
    (B) Yes, we're all OK.
    (C) It was crowded.
    (D) I have a big garden.

21. Mark your answer on your answer sheet.

    (A) It's Jenny's.
    (B) They're not done.
    (C) My new number.
    (D) Those are as well.

22. Mark your answer on your answer sheet.

    (A) Just some gifts.
    (B) Another stamp.
    (C) I always pack light.
    (D) I heard it was.

23. Mark your answer on your answer sheet.

    (A) OK, see you this evening.
    (B) Yes, please help yourself.
    (C) Some paperwork.
    (D) I enjoy walking, too.

24. Mark your answer on your answer sheet.

    (A) A table by the window.
    (B) Let's call our waiter.
    (C) The one on Main Street.
    (D) Half an hour away.

25. Mark your answer on your answer sheet.

    (A) He hasn't called.
    (B) Some books are on display.
    (C) No, the new machines.
    (D) I'll do that this week.

26. Mark your answer on your answer sheet.

    (A) The brown container.
    (B) Please turn left.
    (C) It's mine.
    (D) Usually by bike.

GO ON TO THE NEXT PAGE

LISTENING PART 3

Directions: You will hear some short conversations. You will hear and read two questions about each conversation. Each question has four answer choices. Choose the best answer to each question and mark the letter (A), (B), (C), or (D) on your answer sheet.

27. When will the movie start?
- (A) At four o'clock.
- (B) At five o'clock.
- (C) At six o'clock.
- (D) At seven o'clock.

28. What will the speakers do next?
- (A) Walk to a theater.
- (B) Buy some food.
- (C) Reserve a seat.
- (D) Call some friends.

29. What is the weather like?
- (A) Sunny.
- (B) Windy.
- (C) Rainy.
- (D) Snowy.

30. Where will the speakers go next?
- (A) To an arena.
- (B) To a store.
- (C) To a park.
- (D) To a café.

31. What does the woman want to buy?
- (A) A cake.
- (B) A sweater.
- (C) A purse.
- (D) A coat.

32. What does the man offer to do?
- (A) Check a price.
- (B) Call a manager.
- (C) Wrap a present.
- (D) Make a delivery.

Haysville Library Events

September 5   Writing Workshop
September 12   Book Fair
September 19   Author Reading
September 26   Book Club

Invoice

12 plant supports	$38.45
1 garden scoop	$16.95
6 flower pots	$42.19
18 tomato plants	$29.15

33. Look at the schedule. When will the speakers go to the library?

(A) On September 5.
(B) On September 12.
(C) On September 19.
(D) On September 26.

34. What will the man do?

(A) Write an article.
(B) Get on a bus.
(C) Read a book.
(D) Drive to a library.

35. What does the woman tell the man?

(A) She placed an order.
(B) She planted a garden.
(C) She printed out a coupon.
(D) She broke a pot.

36. Look at the invoice. What amount is incorrect?

(A) $38.45.
(B) $16.95.
(C) $42.19.
(D) $29.15.

GO ON TO THE NEXT PAGE

LISTENING PART 4

Directions: You will hear some short talks. You will hear and read two questions about each talk. Each question has four answer choices. Choose the best answer to each question and mark the letter (A), (B), (C), or (D) on your answer sheet.

37. Who is the speaker?

    (A) A tour guide.

    (B) An instructor.

    (C) A shop owner.

    (D) A new student.

38. What does the speaker want the listeners to do?

    (A) Write down instructions.

    (B) Follow him to a room.

    (C) Read some rules.

    (D) Pass around a test.

---

39. Why is the speaker calling?

    (A) To offer some magazines.

    (B) To ask about a collection.

    (C) To discuss some articles.

    (D) To recommend a book.

40. What does the speaker ask the listener to do?

    (A) Arrange a delivery.

    (B) Correct an error.

    (C) Check her order.

    (D) Return her call.

41. What does the speaker announce?

    (A) The business will close soon.

    (B) The business is twelve years old.

    (C) The business will stay open later.

    (D) The business will be moving.

42. What is happening today?

    (A) A special sale.

    (B) A bike race.

    (C) A board meeting.

    (D) An anniversary party.

43. What is being advertised?

  (A) A travel agency.
  (B) A restaurant.
  (C) A market.
  (D) A hotel.

44. What does the business provide?

  (A) Tourist guidebooks.
  (B) Free transportation.
  (C) Sightseeing tours.
  (D) Beach chairs.

45. Who is the speaker calling?

  (A) A director.
  (B) A salesperson.
  (C) A musician.
  (D) A designer.

46. What does the speaker remind the listener to do?

  (A) Take some photos.
  (B) Try on a costume.
  (C) Bring some drawings.
  (D) Watch a performance.

Schedule		
9:00	Résumés	(Ivan Welch)
11:00	Cover Letters	(Jennifer Rice)
1:00	Finding Jobs	(Ross Collins)
3:00	Interviews	(Nina Reeve)

47. Look at the schedule. Who will speak at eleven o'clock?

  (A) Ivan Welch.
  (B) Jennifer Rice.
  (C) Ross Collins.
  (D) Nina Reeve.

48. What will the speaker do?

  (A) Post some information.
  (B) Call some speakers.
  (C) Repair a vehicle.
  (D) Change his job.

GO ON TO THE NEXT PAGE

Charity Run Courses

Green	8 kilometers
Blue	16 kilometers
Orange	24 kilometers
Red	42 kilometers

49. What time does the speaker want to meet Denise?

(A) 8:00 A.M.
(B) 9:00 A.M.
(C) 10:00 A.M.
(D) 11:00 A.M.

50. Look at the list. Which course will the speaker take?

(A) Green.
(B) Blue.
(C) Orange.
(D) Red.

This is the end of the Listening test. Turn to the Reading test.

READING

This is the Reading test. There are three parts to this test.
You will have 35 minutes to complete the Reading test.

READING PART 1

Directions: You will read some sentences. Each one has a space where a word or phrase is missing. Choose the best answer to complete the sentence. Then mark the letter (A), (B), (C), or (D) on your answer sheet.

Example   Do not _____ on the grass.

(A) find

(B) keep

(C) walk

(D) have

The best answer is (C), so you should mark the letter (C) on your answer sheet.

51. Diane ____ on a purple sweater.

(A) took

(B) made

(C) tried

(D) gave

52. Please sit here ____ you wait.

(A) while

(B) along

(C) since

(D) during

53. Arnold works both quickly ____ carefully.

(A) yet

(B) and

(C) but

(D) also

54. The registration fee is ____ refundable.

(A) fullest

(B) fuller

(C) fully

(D) full

55. Do you know ____ to get to the gallery?

(A) where

(B) what

(C) who

(D) how

GO ON TO THE NEXT PAGE

56. Members must ____ their membership card every year.

(A) renew
(B) renews
(C) renewal
(D) renewing

57. The painters were unable to finish the job ____ .

(A) completely
(B) completion
(C) completes
(D) complete

58. The entrance was too ____ for the sofa to fit through.

(A) clear
(B) narrow
(C) close
(D) stuck

59. February and March were ____ than usual this year.

(A) warm
(B) warms
(C) warmer
(D) warmest

60. Water and light snacks will be ____ during the tour.

(A) continued
(B) reached
(C) offered
(D) attached

61. Wang Lei always orders a ____ size coffee and a donut.

(A) regular
(B) regulars
(C) regularly
(D) regularity

62. Andrea has been promoted ____ sales clerk to store manager.

(A) for
(B) until
(C) before
(D) from

63. The soccer team will strengthen its skills by ____ every day.

(A) practice
(B) to practice
(C) practicing
(D) practiced

64. You do not have to mark all the tests by ____ .

(A) yours
(B) your
(C) you
(D) yourself

65. ____ author Erik Rodgers tomorrow for a discussion about his book.

(A) Appear
(B) Listen
(C) Connect
(D) Join

READING PART 2

Directions: You will read some short texts. Each one has three spaces where a word, phrase, or sentence is missing. For each space, choose the best answer to complete the text. Then mark the letter (A), (B), (C), or (D) on your answer sheet.

Example

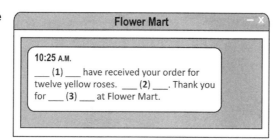

1. (A) We
   (B) Us
   (C) Our
   (D) Ours

2. (A) Please ask for help.
   (B) Red is a bright color.
   (C) They will arrive today.
   (D) Put them on my desk.

3. (A) shop
   (B) shops
   (C) shopped
   (D) shopping

The best answer for question 1 is (A), so you should mark the letter (A) on your answer sheet.

The best answer for question 2 is (C), so you should mark the letter (C) on your answer sheet.

The best answer for question 3 is (D), so you should mark the letter (D) on your answer sheet.

GO ON TO THE NEXT PAGE

Jamie [4:29 P.M.]

Hi Sandra. There's a new art __(66)__ at the gallery. My friend
and I will __(67)__ there tomorrow. Do you want to come with
__(68)__? Please let me know.

66. (A) technique
    (B) exhibit
    (C) magazine
    (D) class

67. (A) have
    (B) do
    (C) see
    (D) go

68. (A) them
    (B) you
    (C) us
    (D) it

Questions 69–71 refer to the following notice.

ATTENTION

The bakery will be closed on June 18. This is __(69)__ we will be
replacing our ovens. If you would like to buy some __(70)__ that
day, please stop by our Bridge Street location. We __(71)__ for
any inconvenience.

69. (A) whether
    (B) unless
    (C) though
    (D) because

70. (A) bread
    (B) paper
    (C) wood
    (D) jewelry

71. (A) understand
    (B) apologize
    (C) accept
    (D) excuse

GO ON TO THE NEXT PAGE

Questions 72–74 refer to the following advertisement.

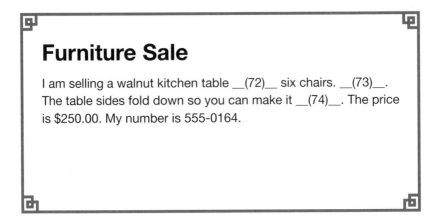

Furniture Sale

I am selling a walnut kitchen table __(72)__ six chairs. __(73)__.
The table sides fold down so you can make it __(74)__. The price
is $250.00. My number is 555-0164.

72. (A) with
    (B) over
    (C) among
    (D) from

73. (A) The dining room was cleaned.
    (B) My coworker bought some.
    (C) Please have a seat anywhere.
    (D) They are in excellent condition.

74. (A) nearer
    (B) quicker
    (C) smaller
    (D) easier

Questions 75–77 refer to the following label.

Mixtex Maintenance

With proper cleaning, your Mixtex blender will __(75)__ operate smoothly. After use, take the device apart. __(76)__. Be careful! The blades are sharp and can cause injury if not __(77)__ with care. For more maintenance information, please see the user manual.

75. (A) ever
(B) always
(C) most
(D) still

76. (A) Some of these might be missing.
(B) That is how you can make smoothies.
(C) They are sold in five separate colors.
(D) Then wash each part with detergent.

77. (A) handles
(B) handling
(C) handled
(D) handler

GO ON TO THE NEXT PAGE

● ● ○

To:	Miguel Sanchez
From:	Jody Goodwin
Date:	November 9
Subject:	Appointment

Dear Mr. Sanchez,

This message is __(78)__ you about your appointment tomorrow. The doctor will see you at two o'clock. __(79)__. That will give you time to fill out a medical history form. If you have __(80)__ questions beforehand, feel free to call us.

Best regards,

Jody Goodwin
York Health Clinic

78. (A) to remind
(B) reminded
(C) reminder
(D) reminds

79. (A) The waiting room is crowded.
(B) We are sorry for the delay.
(C) Please arrive 20 minutes early.
(D) The clinic has more facilities.

80. (A) those
(B) any
(C) all
(D) either

READING PART 3

Directions: You will read some texts such as notices, letters, and instant messages. Each text is followed by two or three questions. Choose the best answer to each question and mark the letter (A), (B), (C), or (D) on your answer sheet.

Example

Milltown Supermarket

We have the freshest fruit and vegetables in town!

Opening Hours
Monday to Friday, 9:00 A.M. to 9:00 P.M.
Saturday and Sunday, 10:00 A.M. to 7:00 P.M.

1. What does the store sell?

(A) Food

(B) Clothing

(C) Books

(D) Furniture

2. What time does the store close on Tuesday?

(A) At 7:00 P.M.

(B) At 8:00 P.M.

(C) At 9:00 P.M.

(D) At 10:00 P.M.

The best answer for question 1 is (A), so you should mark the letter (A) on your answer sheet.

The best answer for question 2 is (C), so you should mark the letter (C) on your answer sheet.

GO ON TO THE NEXT PAGE

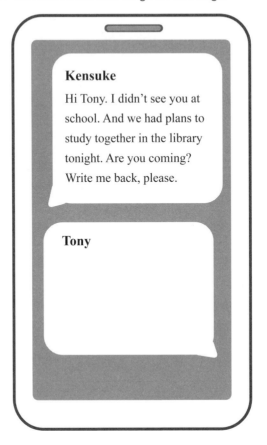

Kensuke

Hi Tony. I didn't see you at school. And we had plans to study together in the library tonight. Are you coming? Write me back, please.

Tony

81. Who most likely are the writers?

(A) Librarians
(B) Classmates
(C) Relatives
(D) Coworkers

82. Select the best response to Kensuke's message.

(A) "Yes, it arrived late."
(B) "I've already read that."
(C) "Sorry, I have the flu."
(D) "Never on Thursdays."

Sunburst Dry Cleaners

Customer name: Jeremy Harris

Phone number: 555-0146

Date and time of drop off: October 8 (6:28 p.m.)

Date requested for pick up: October 10

Item/Service	Quantity	Rate	Amount
Shirt	2	$ 3.20	$ 6.40
Pants	1	$ 5.50	$ 5.50
Zipper replacement	1	$ 7.80	$ 7.80
		Subtotal	$ 19.70
		Tax	$ 1.58
		Total	$ 21.28

83. What did Mr. Harris plan to do on October 10?

(A) Deliver some shirts
(B) Pick out a jacket
(C) Collect some clothing
(D) Buy some suit pants

84. What will probably be removed?

(A) A zipper
(B) A stain
(C) A button
(D) A tag

GO ON TO THE NEXT PAGE

Landscaping Work in May

Several trees will soon be planted around the parking lot. The work will occur between May 6 and 12. Throughout the period, tenants who park in row A or K should park someplace else. This will ensure that their cars do not get damaged. Please also note that the guest spots will be open to everyone at that time.

Greyson Tower Management

85. Who is the notice for?

(A) Landscaping workers
(B) Delivery drivers
(C) Property managers
(D) Building tenants

86. What will change on May 6?

(A) A garden of vegetables
(B) An arrangement of cars
(C) A rule for guests
(D) A fee for a service

Questions 87–88 refer to the following text message.

Kristi

Ramon, friends of mine are coming to town next month. They want to see a play. You go to the theater a lot. Have you seen anything recently that you can recommend?

Ramon

There's an excellent comedy at the Avenue Theater. It's so popular that tickets sell out about a week before each show.

Kristi

87. What does Kristi want from Ramon?

(A) A review
(B) A suggestion
(C) Some dates
(D) Some directions

88. Select the best response to Ramon's message.

(A) "Well, we practiced very hard."
(B) "Yes, we're really enjoying it."
(C) "What time will it be on TV?"
(D) "Oh, I'd better get them soon!"

GO ON TO THE NEXT PAGE

Arlington Hotel Reservations

If you wish to cancel your reservation, please do so at least 48 hours before the date we expected you to arrive. We will then provide a full refund. If your cancellation is made within 48 hours prior to the date, you will be charged for one night. To change the date of your booking, please call our front desk.

89. What is described on the Web page?

(A) A cancellation policy
(B) A registration method
(C) A hotel restaurant
(D) A check-in procedure

90. According to the Web page, what can the hotel do?

(A) Store some luggage
(B) Reduce some charges
(C) Return a payment
(D) Change a room

91. Why should people call the front desk?

(A) To get an explanation
(B) To change a reservation
(C) To report a mistake
(D) To ask for an extension

Questions 92–94 refer to the following advertisement.

Montgomery Park

Montgomery Park is a zoo with more than 800 different animals. On August 2, we will celebrate our 20th anniversary. On that day only, you can visit at no charge! Come and see our beautiful animals. Also, enjoy the outdoor activities we have planned just for special day. To find out more, visit our Web site. And while you are there, you can also view recordings of our staff feeding the animals.

TEST 1

TEST 2

TEST 3

92. What will happen on August 2?

(A) A park will reopen.
(B) A speech will be given.
(C) Admission will be free.
(D) Pictures will be displayed.

93. What is stated about the special activities?

(A) They include feeding animals.
(B) They will take place outside.
(C) They will begin at 9:00 A.M.
(D) They are held every weekend.

94. What can people do on the Web site?

(A) Download pictures
(B) Read about ingredients
(C) Look at a map
(D) Watch some videos

GO ON TO THE NEXT PAGE

Questions 95–97 refer to the following online chat conversation.

 Janine's Messages

Doug   [4:37 P.M.]

Hi, Janine. I was hoping to finish your walls this afternoon. I'm done in the kitchen, but parts of the dining room will have to wait.

Janine   [4:39 P.M.]

Oh, is the cabinet still in the way? I thought I'd moved it far enough away from the walls.

Doug   [4:41 P.M.]

No, it's fine where it is. Thanks for your help. Actually, I ran out of the light blue paint you want me to use on the window frames. I'll get a can at a store tomorrow.

Janine   [4:43 P.M.]

OK, but remember, only one place sells that type. It's the store on Cornell Street.

---

95. What does Doug want to finish?

(A) Preparing some meals
(B) Hanging some pictures
(C) Painting some walls
(D) Installing some lights

96. What is NOT mentioned about Janine?

(A) She bought a can.
(B) She moved furniture.
(C) She has a dining room.
(D) She wants light blue paint.

97. What does Janine remind Doug about?

(A) A business has moved.
(B) A cabinet is an antique.
(C) Two frames are wooden.
(D) Only one store sells a product.

Questions 98–100 refer to the following article.

Best Hot Dogs in Town

Brian Trang's homemade hot dogs are delicious. When he opened his stand a year ago, he did not believe it would ever be very successful. In fact, it was a huge surprise to him when it became so well known. He parks the stand beside Rays Stadium. "It's a great location," he said. "It's busy whenever there's a baseball game. The area is popular with visitors from other countries, too." Mr. Trang said he will join this year's Best Hot Dog Contest. As for other future plans, he commented: "I'll set up another stand or two. Maybe I'll even open my own restaurant someday."

98. What surprised Mr. Trang?

(A) The success of his business
(B) The requests of his customers
(C) The results of a game
(D) The number of visitors

99. What is Mr. Trang planning to do?

(A) Join a sporting event
(B) Hand out a recipe
(C) Enter a competition
(D) Travel overseas

100. What does Mr. Trang suggest?

(A) He will sell his business.
(B) He will expand his business.
(C) He has changed a menu.
(D) He has won some awards.

Stop! This is the end of the Reading test. If you finish before time is called, you may go back to Reading Parts 1, 2 and 3 and check your work.

第 2 回テスト

TEST 2

解答・解説は
.... 別冊 76 - 143 ページ

🔘 音声ファイル

トラック名
PART 1: T2_P1_Dir ▶ T2_P1_Q6
PART 2: T2_P2_Dir ▶ T2_P2_Q26
PART 3: T2_P3_Dir ▶ T2_P3_Q35-36
PART 4: T2_P4_Dir ▶ T2_P4_Q49-50

LISTENING

This is the Listening test. There are four parts to this test.

LISTENING PART 1

Directions: You will see a set of four pictures in your test book, and you will hear one short phrase or sentence. Look at the set of pictures. Choose the picture that the phrase or sentence best describes. Then mark the letter (A), (B), (C), or (D) on your answer sheet.

Look at the sample pictures below and listen to the phrase.

Example

You will hear: A man wearing headphones.

(A)

(B)

(C)

(D)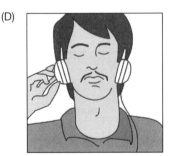

The best answer is (D), so you should mark the letter (D) on your answer sheet.

1. (A)  (B)

(C)  (D)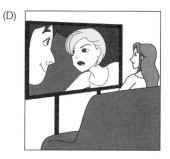

2. (A)  (B)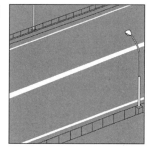

(C)  (D)

GO ON TO THE NEXT PAGE

3. (A)

(B)

(C)

(D)

4. (A)

(B)

(C)

(D)

5. (A)  (B)

(C)  (D)

6. (A) 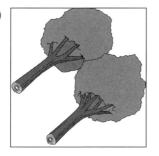 (B)

(C)  (D)

GO ON TO THE NEXT PAGE

LISTENING PART 2

Directions: You will hear some questions or statements. After each question or statement, you will hear and read four responses. Choose the best response to each question or statement. Then mark the letter (A), (B), (C), or (D) on your answer sheet.

Now listen to a sample question.

Example

You will hear: What time is it?

You will hear and read   (A) It's three o'clock.

(B) Several times.

(C) Near the hotel.

(D) Yes, it is.

The best answer is (A), so you should mark the letter (A) on your answer sheet.

7. Mark your answer on your answer sheet.

(A) A bigger building.
(B) After I find an apartment.
(C) A moving company.
(D) To the supermarket.

8. Mark your answer on your answer sheet.

(A) Your appointment.
(B) About two hours.
(C) No, there aren't any.
(D) Oh, I can do that.

9. Mark your answer on your answer sheet.

(A) I'll take it for you.
(B) A winter coat.
(C) Your locker key.
(D) She's over there.

10. Mark your answer on your answer sheet.

(A) Several times.
(B) Near the university.
(C) I didn't see it.
(D) It's at seven o'clock.

11. Mark your answer on your answer sheet.

(A) Yes, they did.
(B) It's been reduced.
(C) I'd be happy to.
(D) Meet me at seven.

12. Mark your answer on your answer sheet.

(A) Warmer clothes.
(B) They look great!
(C) I'll bring more tea.
(D) I haven't read it.

13. Mark your answer on your answer sheet.

(A) Not quite enough.
(B) Usually at lunch time.
(C) It was very interesting.
(D) Yes, I did it yesterday.

14. Mark your answer on your answer sheet.

(A) I'll just have water.
(B) In the dining room.
(C) A few more glasses.
(D) A dollar eighty.

15. Mark your answer on your answer sheet.

(A) Next to the door.
(B) My cousin did.
(C) The sun came out.
(D) The black one, please.

GO ON TO THE NEXT PAGE

16. Mark your answer on your answer sheet.

    (A) All sorts of dishes.
    (B) You're right, they are.
    (C) A lot of them.
    (D) It's pretty hot.

17. Mark your answer on your answer sheet.

    (A) We'll make more of it.
    (B) I'm going to the countryside.
    (C) By train is best.
    (D) I'd be delighted to.

18. Mark your answer on your answer sheet.

    (A) Sometimes by bus.
    (B) Late last night.
    (C) From the library.
    (D) He's not feeling well.

19. Mark your answer on your answer sheet.

    (A) By bicycle.
    (B) A sales representative.
    (C) Mostly antiques.
    (D) At a delivery service.

20. Mark your answer on your answer sheet.

    (A) Check the coffee table.
    (B) I have change.
    (C) No, they weren't.
    (D) A glass is fine.

21. Mark your answer on your answer sheet.

    (A) They'll arrive tomorrow.
    (B) Only recently.
    (C) Yes, I know how.
    (D) The blue car.

22. Mark your answer on your answer sheet.

(A) Until Sunday morning.
(B) Sometime next year.
(C) Yes, I do.
(D) I'm sure it'll be lovely.

23. Mark your answer on your answer sheet.

(A) No, the sixth aisle.
(B) I need some medicine.
(C) With Dr. Philips.
(D) Yes, I asked the receptionist.

24. Mark your answer on your answer sheet.

(A) We watched it today.
(B) That's a good offer.
(C) At the shopping center.
(D) No, we shouldn't forget.

25. Mark your answer on your answer sheet.

(A) I took a taxi instead.
(B) Twenty minutes by train.
(C) The deadline has passed.
(D) A different route.

26. Mark your answer on your answer sheet.

(A) Both of them did.
(B) It's delicious!
(C) Yes, I brought some, too.
(D) The bakery across the street.

GO ON TO THE NEXT PAGE

LISTENING PART 3

Directions: You will hear some short conversations. You will hear and read two questions about each conversation. Each question has four answer choices. Choose the best answer to each question and mark the letter (A), (B), (C), or (D) on your answer sheet.

27. What did the man do yesterday?

(A) He watched a game.
(B) He played a sport.
(C) He saw a surfer.
(D) He joined a gym.

28. When does the woman go surfing?

(A) On Thursdays.
(B) On Fridays.
(C) On Saturdays.
(D) On Sundays.

29. Where are the speakers?

(A) At a supermarket.
(B) At a travel agency.
(C) At a restaurant.
(D) At a hair salon.

30. What will the woman do next?

(A) Follow a waiter.
(B) Check her schedule.
(C) Make an appointment.
(D) Move some tables.

31. What does the woman ask about?

(A) A train departure.
(B) A registration deadline.
(C) A school club.
(D) A seminar topic.

32. Where did the woman put her calendar?

(A) On a wall.
(B) By a door.
(C) On a desk.
(D) In a drawer.

TV Shows (7:00 p.m.)

Kitchen Kings	Cooking
Northern Stars	Movie
Today's World	News
Doctor Elliot	Series

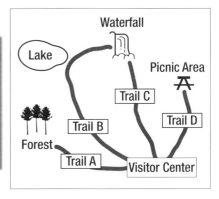

33. Look at the TV listing. What will the speakers watch?

(A) *Kitchen Kings.*
(B) *Northern Stars.*
(C) *Today's World.*
(D) *Doctor Elliot.*

34. What does the woman plan to do?

(A) Prepare for a trip.
(B) Try on a business suit.
(C) Record a program.
(D) Change the channel.

35. Look at the map. Which trail will the man probably take?

(A) Trail A.
(B) Trail B.
(C) Trail C.
(D) Trail D.

36. What will the man do with his friends?

(A) Cycling.
(B) Jogging.
(C) Camping.
(D) Fishing.

GO ON TO THE NEXT PAGE

LISTENING PART 4

Directions: You will hear some short talks. You will hear and read two questions about each talk. Each question has four answer choices. Choose the best answer to each question and mark the letter (A), (B), (C), or (D) on your answer sheet.

37. Where is the announcement being made?

(A) On a train.
(B) On an airplane.
(C) In a travel agency.
(D) At an airline counter.

38. What are the listeners instructed to do?

(A) Check a name.
(B) Review a menu.
(C) Watch a video.
(D) Ask a question.

39. What is the speaker's problem?

(A) She is very tired.
(B) She will be late.
(C) She lost a phone.
(D) She forgot a book.

40. What does the speaker ask Kathy to do?

(A) Send an address.
(B) Give her a ride.
(C) Schedule an appointment.
(D) Move some paper.

41. What type of business did the listener call?

(A) A hotel.
(B) An airline.
(C) A travel agency.
(D) A book store.

42. According to the speaker, what can listeners do on a Web site?

(A) Make a reservation.
(B) Download a coupon.
(C) Read some reviews.
(D) See some photos.

43. What is most likely being
advertised?

(A) Some office spaces.
(B) Some new products.
(C) A remodeling company.
(D) An apartment building.

44. What does the speaker say will
happen?

(A) A name will change.
(B) A station will open.
(C) A contract will expire.
(D) A tour will end.

45. Where most likely are the
listeners?

(A) At a museum.
(B) At a restaurant.
(C) At an electronics shop.
(D) At a concert hall.

46. According to the speaker,
what will the listeners be able
to do?

(A) Ask some questions.
(B) Play an instrument.
(C) Listen to recordings.
(D) Keep some headphones.

Weather Forecast

Tuesday:	Cool
Wednesday:	Humid
Thursday:	Hot
Friday:	Warm

47. Look at the forecast. Which day
was the event scheduled for?

(A) Tuesday.
(B) Wednesday.
(C) Thursday.
(D) Friday.

48. What does the speaker ask
the listener to do?

(A) Clean up an office.
(B) Arrange a meeting.
(C) Cancel the event.
(D) Contact volunteers.

GO ON TO THE NEXT PAGE

Training Schedule (Day 1)

10:00 A.M.	Safety
11:00 A.M.	Tools
1:00 P.M.	Menu
3:00 P.M.	Procedures

49. What were the listeners hired to do?

(A) Take orders.
(B) Prepare food.
(C) Help receptionists.
(D) Arrange tables.

50. Look at the schedule. When will the manager start her session?

(A) At 10:00 A.M.
(B) At 11:00 A.M.
(C) At 1:00 P.M.
(D) At 3:00 P.M.

This is the end of the Listening test. Turn to the Reading test.

READING

This is the Reading test. There are three parts to this test.
You will have 35 minutes to complete the Reading test.

READING PART 1

Directions: You will read some sentences. Each one has a space where a word or phrase is missing. Choose the best answer to complete the sentence. Then mark the letter (A), (B), (C), or (D) on your answer sheet.

Example   Do not _____ on the grass.

(A) find

(B) keep

(C) walk

(D) have

The best answer is (C), so you should mark the letter (C) on your answer sheet.

51. My roommate ____ several bills this month.

(A) receive

(B) to receive

(C) received

(D) receiving

52. Gina ____ the costume on October 25.

(A) created

(B) creating

(C) creatively

(D) creation

53. All students must ____ their assignment by Friday.

(A) achieve

(B) put

(C) apply

(D) submit

54. ____ starting his own company, Jim was a waiter.

(A) Also

(B) Before

(C) Within

(D) Instead

55. The cook spread out the dough ____ on the tray.

(A) flatten

(B) flatness

(C) flatly

(D) flattening

GO ON TO THE NEXT PAGE

56. You should be proud of ____ for passing the exam.

(A) you
(B) yours
(C) your
(D) yourself

57. Although the climb was ____, Akiko went to the top of the mountain.

(A) danger
(B) dangerous
(C) dangerously
(D) dangers

58. After working in Australia, Li Yueh ____ to Taiwan.

(A) began
(B) returned
(C) visited
(D) planned

59. Does anyone know ____ channel the tournament is on?

(A) what
(B) where
(C) when
(D) why

60. Rachel prepared the main course and dessert ____ .

(A) separated
(B) separating
(C) separately
(D) separation

61. Auditions for the show are taking place ____ afternoon today.

(A) all
(B) each
(C) whole
(D) every

62. No one ____ the director can sign a contract.

(A) among
(B) apart
(C) except
(D) other

63. You can purchase tickets daily ____ a one-week pass.

(A) so
(B) if
(C) but
(D) or

64. Many houses ____ electric power during the storm.

(A) fell
(B) kept
(C) missed
(D) lost

65. The scientists agreed that the research project had gone

____ .

(A) smoothen
(B) smoothly
(C) smoother
(D) smooth

READING PART 2

Directions: You will read some short texts. Each one has three spaces where a word, phrase, or sentence is missing. For each space, choose the best answer to complete the text. Then mark the letter (A), (B), (C), or (D) on your answer sheet.

Example

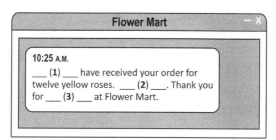

1. (A) We
   (B) Us
   (C) Our
   (D) Ours

2. (A) Please ask for help.
   (B) Red is a bright color.
   (C) They will arrive today.
   (D) Put them on my desk.

3. (A) shop
   (B) shops
   (C) shopped
   (D) shopping

The best answer for question 1 is (A), so you should mark the letter (A) on your answer sheet.

The best answer for question 2 is (C), so you should mark the letter (C) on your answer sheet.

The best answer for question 3 is (D), so you should mark the letter (D) on your answer sheet.

GO ON TO THE NEXT PAGE

Questions 66–68 refer to the following text message.

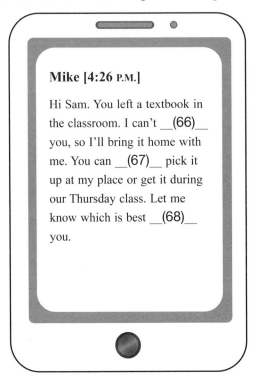

Mike [4:26 P.M.]

Hi Sam. You left a textbook in the classroom. I can't __(66)__ you, so I'll bring it home with me. You can __(67)__ pick it up at my place or get it during our Thursday class. Let me know which is best __(68)__ you.

66. (A) found
(B) to find
(C) finding
(D) find

67. (A) both
(B) either
(C) whether
(D) each

68. (A) for
(B) to
(C) of
(D) from

Ironing Instructions

For a smooth surface, iron this tablecloth after washing __(69)__ in cold water. The material should be ironed before it is __(70)__ dry. We also __(71)__ using a high heat setting and the iron's steam function.

69. (A) it
  (B) one
  (C) either
  (D) another

70. (A) complete
  (B) completely
  (C) completing
  (D) completion

71. (A) believe
  (B) remember
  (C) instruct
  (D) recommend

Questions 72–74 refer to the following e-mail.

To:	Kyle Rhodes
From:	Marissa Zhao
Date:	July 6
Subject:	Lunch

Hello Kyle.

I can't meet you for lunch today. __(72)__. So, I agreed to take his shift. We could meet tomorrow instead. I'll be free all day __(73)__ my five o'clock aerobics class. I'm sorry about __(74)__.

Marissa

72. (A) I'm not very hungry.
    (B) Take-out is available.
    (C) It's on Walnut Street.
    (D) My coworker is sick.

73. (A) over
    (B) before
    (C) onto
    (D) during

74. (A) cancelling
    (B) staying
    (C) forgetting
    (D) leaving

Gallery News

The Francis Art Gallery __(75)__ a new autumn exhibit yesterday. It features fourteen sculptures by Carmen Gray. __(76)__. His works have been shown in many museums worldwide. The new exhibit will be on __(77)__ until the end of November.

75. (A) opens
   (B) is open
   (C) opened
   (D) will open

76. (A) Both will arrive tomorrow.
   (B) This will be his first show.
   (C) He is a well-known artist.
   (D) Everyone loved the film.

77. (A) watch
   (B) display
   (C) show
   (D) outlook

GO ON TO THE NEXT PAGE

Sailor Sam's offers a __(78)__ range of boats for rent in Capeville. __(79)__ you want a small sailboat or a big yacht, we have what you are looking for. Our business also runs different boat tours. __(80)__. For bookings, call 555-0139.

78. (A) widen
(B) width
(C) wide
(D) widely

79. (A) Although
(B) Because
(C) While
(D) Whether

80. (A) Weather permitting, the trips are made daily.
(B) We hope you will attend tomorrow's event.
(C) Our flight details have been sent by e-mail.
(D) Ferry passengers can expect delays this week.

READING PART 3

Directions: You will read some texts such as notices, letters, and instant messages. Each text is followed by two or three questions. Choose the best answer to each question and mark the letter (A), (B), (C), or (D) on your answer sheet.

Example

Milltown Supermarket

We have the freshest fruit and vegetables in town!

Opening Hours
Monday to Friday, 9:00 A.M. to 9:00 P.M.
Saturday and Sunday, 10:00 A.M. to 7:00 P.M.

1. What does the store sell?

(A) Food

(B) Clothing

(C) Books

(D) Furniture

2. What time does the store close on Tuesday?

(A) At 7:00 P.M.

(B) At 8:00 P.M.

(C) At 9:00 P.M.

(D) At 10:00 P.M.

The best answer for question 1 is (A), so you should mark the letter (A) on your answer sheet.

The best answer for question 2 is (C), so you should mark the letter (C) on your answer sheet.

GO ON TO THE NEXT PAGE

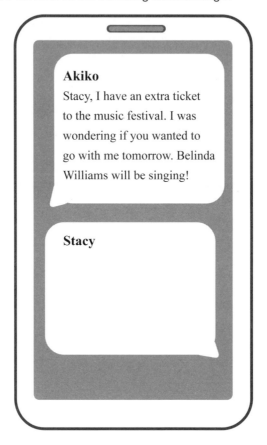

Akiko

Stacy, I have an extra ticket to the music festival. I was wondering if you wanted to go with me tomorrow. Belinda Williams will be singing!

Stacy

81. What will Akiko probably do tomorrow?

(A) Watch a performance
(B) Listen to an album
(C) Sell some tickets
(D) Play an instrument

82. Select the best response to Akiko's message.

(A) "Of course I told them."
(B) "Does she think so?"
(C) "Yes, I heard her clearly."
(D) "I'd love to go, thanks!"

Questions 83–84 refer to the following information.

Information for Visitors

A membership card is all you need to take out a book. First, search our catalog for the item you want. Next, write down the call number you see there and then locate the book on our shelves. Finally, check out the item at the front desk.

83. What does the information explain?

   (A) When a library is open
   (B) Who to ask for assistance
   (C) How to borrow a book
   (D) Where to make a purchase

84. Why should people check a catalog?

   (A) To see some pictures
   (B) To find a number
   (C) To read a review
   (D) To search for a sale

GO ON TO THE NEXT PAGE

Questions 85–86 refer to the following text message.

Tony

Good news! My supervisor rearranged my schedule at the grocery store. Starting this week, I won't be working on Saturdays anymore. I can join your baseball team.

Aaron

That is good news! We really need another player. I'll let everyone know. Our next practice will be at Highland Park this week.

Tony

85. Why is Tony happy?

(A) He was hired for a job.
(B) He will take a vacation.
(C) His favorite team won.
(D) His schedule changed.

86. Select the best response to Aaron's message.

(A) "Probably by bicycle."
(B) "OK, I'll be there."
(C) "Thanks for coming!"
(D) "They all played well."

T&M Professionals
45 Ellis Road,
Victoria, V8W 2C2,
Canada

Invoice: #79345

Invoice date: February 12

Client:

Adventure Tours & Travel 2757 Wharf Street, V8W 3H9 Victoria, Canada

Description of service:

Washing windows and walls on February 10: $218.00
Carpet shampooing on February 11: $375.00

Subtotal: $593.00
Tax (12%): $71.16
Total: $664.16
Payment due by: February 19

Thank you for choosing T&M!

87. What does T&M Professionals provide?

(A) Travel services
(B) Construction services
(C) Decorating services
(D) Cleaning services

88. When does the total charge have to be paid?

(A) By February 10
(B) By February 11
(C) By February 12
(D) By February 19

GO ON TO THE NEXT PAGE

Questions 89–91 refer to the following Web page.

https://www.champssuperstore.com/news

Exciting News!

Our annual spring sale will start on Saturday. Every winter, we fill our stores with brand-new merchandise. At the end of the season, we make room for summer items. So, from March 20 to April 3, we will be offering big discounts on skis, snowboards, and skates. To find a Champs Superstore near you, see the About page of this Web site.

89. What does the business do in the winter?

(A) It makes more space.
(B) It hires extra staff.
(C) It holds a competition.
(D) It stays open later.

90. What will NOT be on sale?

(A) Skis
(B) Snowboards
(C) Shoes
(D) Skates

91. How can people find a store location?

(A) By calling a salesperson
(B) By visiting another page
(C) By checking a mall directory
(D) By entering an address

Discovery on Sycamore Avenue

PALMETTO, May 19 — A local resident recently found something interesting in his garden. While planting flowers, he dug up a very old bowl. Jack Lawrence, who made the discovery, said: "I thought it was a rock. Then I realized it was filled with dirt. After I got that out, I saw that I was holding a bowl." According to the Palmetto Museum, native people made the bowl three thousand years ago. Mr. Lawrence donated it to the museum, where it is now on display.

---

92. What is the article mainly about?

(A) An ancient container
(B) A vegetarian dish
(C) A gardening project
(D) An antique market

93. What did Mr. Lawrence suggest?

(A) He broke a rock.
(B) He lost a shovel.
(C) He removed some dirt.
(D) He sent some flowers.

94. What is stated about the museum?

(A) It opened three years ago.
(B) It will increase a fee.
(C) It is often crowded.
(D) It set up a display.

GO ON TO THE NEXT PAGE

Questions 95–97 refer to the following notice.

Public Notice

The Marzetta Bridge will be closed for the 62nd Daffodil Parade today, which begins at 11:00 A.M. If you are planning to drive in or out of downtown Jerrell City, we recommend using Harrods Street. Traffic will also not be permitted on Wilkinson Road, which will be the route for the event. Metered parking along Branson Avenue is available. Additionally, the convention hall on Apple Boulevard is charging its usual fee of $20.00 for all-day parking. To ensure you get a space, you should arrive at least one hour before the parade begins. Drivers should also expect traffic delays throughout the day.

95. According to the notice, what will be closed?

(A) A shop
(B) A road
(C) A park
(D) A hall

96. Where will the parade be held?

(A) On Harrods Street
(B) On Wilkinson Road
(C) On Branson Avenue
(D) On Apple Boulevard

97. What are people advised to do?

(A) Arrive by 10:00 A.M.
(B) Buy tickets at 11:00 A.M.
(C) Read some instructions
(D) Listen for traffic updates

Questions **98–100** refer to the following online chat conversation.

 Miguel's Messages

Arlene [3:26 P.M.]
Miguel, I'm in my room on the ninth floor. I can't connect to the wireless Internet. Have you tried to?

Miguel [3:27 P.M.]
Yes, but it's not working here either. When I called the front desk, they told me the problem will be fixed by tonight.

Arlene [3:28 P.M.]
OK. Are you hungry? There's a pizzeria across the street. I can read their big sign from my window. It says they offer free Internet access.

Miguel [3:29 P.M.]
Great. We'll go online there and check what sightseeing spots we can visit tomorrow. Let's meet in the lobby at six.

98. Why does Arlene write to Miguel?

(A) To request a password
(B) To ask about a problem
(C) To ask for directions
(D) To explain a decision

99. What does Arlene say she can see?

(A) A menu
(B) A wire
(C) A sign
(D) A tool

100. Why will Arlene and Miguel meet at six o'clock?

(A) They will make a complaint.
(B) They will have a meal.
(C) They will do online shopping.
(D) They will watch a movie.

Stop! This is the end of the Reading test. If you finish before time is called, you may go back to Reading Parts 1, 2 and 3 and check your work.

第 3 回テスト

TEST 3

解答・解説は

▶ 音声ファイル

トラック名
PART 1: T3_P1_Dir ▶ T3_P1_Q6
PART 2: T3_P2_Dir ▶ T3_P2_Q26
PART 3: T3_P3_Dir ▶ T3_P3_Q35-36
PART 4: T3_P4_Dir ▶ T3_P4_Q49-50

LISTENING

This is the Listening test. There are four parts to this test.

LISTENING PART 1

Directions: You will see a set of four pictures in your test book, and you will hear one short phrase or sentence. Look at the set of pictures. Choose the picture that the phrase or sentence best describes. Then mark the letter (A), (B), (C), or (D) on your answer sheet.

Look at the sample pictures below and listen to the phrase.

Example

You will hear: A man wearing headphones.

(A)
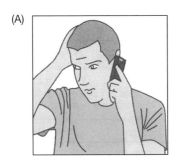

(B)

(C)

(D)
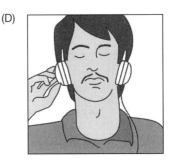

The best answer is (D), so you should mark the letter (D) on your answer sheet.

1. (A)

(B)

(C)

(D)

2. (A)

(B)

(C)

(D)

GO ON TO THE NEXT PAGE

3. (A)  (B)

(C)  (D)

4. (A)  (B)

(C)  (D)

5. (A)  (B)

(C)  (D)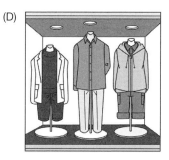

6. (A)  (B)

(C)  (D)

GO ON TO THE NEXT PAGE

LISTENING PART 2

Directions: You will hear some questions or statements. After each question or statement, you will hear and read four responses. Choose the best response to each question or statement. Then mark the letter (A), (B), (C), or (D) on your answer sheet.

Now listen to a sample question.

Example

You will hear: What time is it?

You will hear and read   (A) It's three o'clock.

                                  (B) Several times.

                                  (C) Near the hotel.

                                  (D) Yes, it is.

The best answer is (A), so you should mark the letter (A) on your answer sheet.

7. Mark your answer on your answer sheet.

    (A) A window seat.
    (B) It leaves at seven.
    (C) Earlier is better.
    (D) It was long.

8. Mark your answer on your answer sheet.

    (A) Yes, that's correct.
    (B) It's my school.
    (C) Hong Kong, I think.
    (D) She just called.

9. Mark your answer on your answer sheet.

    (A) Sure, help yourself.
    (B) You, too.
    (C) Yeah, we're fine.
    (D) The new printer.

10. Mark your answer on your answer sheet.

    (A) On 22nd Street.
    (B) I love summer.
    (C) This is cheaper.
    (D) In early January.

11. Mark your answer on your answer sheet.

    (A) No, not usually.
    (B) See you on Thursday.
    (C) Oh, I'm sorry.
    (D) All the way home.

12. Mark your answer on your answer sheet.

    (A) He's at work now.
    (B) It isn't over there.
    (C) Sixteen years old.
    (D) He practices daily.

13. Mark your answer on your answer sheet.

    (A) Over thirty euros.
    (B) I decided to fly.
    (C) No, it's sunny now.
    (D) Thank you so much.

14. Mark your answer on your answer sheet.

    (A) You're welcome.
    (B) About ten times already.
    (C) Everyone in my science class.
    (D) Next Saturday.

15. Mark your answer on your answer sheet.

    (A) From a travel agent.
    (B) Have as many as you want.
    (C) After that, turn right.
    (D) Mary said she would.

GO ON TO THE NEXT PAGE

16. Mark your answer on your answer sheet.

   (A) Yes, please wrap them.
   (B) Next to the sofa.
   (C) Oh, what's in it?
   (D) Of course it is.

17. Mark your answer on your answer sheet.

   (A) Go ahead, take some.
   (B) The big ones?
   (C) I also tried some.
   (D) No, not at all.

18. Mark your answer on your answer sheet.

   (A) The bag over there.
   (B) Actually, we all did.
   (C) She said she's OK.
   (D) A minute before you.

19. Mark your answer on your answer sheet.

   (A) I did this morning.
   (B) I totally agree.
   (C) A nearby hospital.
   (D) I've never tried that.

20. Mark your answer on your answer sheet.

   (A) Check the kitchen counter.
   (B) Yes, twenty dollars.
   (C) The painting is on the wall.
   (D) To pick up a pizza.

21. Mark your answer on your answer sheet.

   (A) Don't worry, I will.
   (B) An hour ago.
   (C) That's my cousin's.
   (D) For a short trip.

22. Mark your answer on your answer sheet.

    (A) No, they won't mind.
    (B) Just tea, thanks.
    (C) We ordered too many.
    (D) Let's go out.

23. Mark your answer on your answer sheet.

    (A) That's exactly right.
    (B) I got it from the library.
    (C) About starting a business.
    (D) Two bookings.

24. Mark your answer on your answer sheet.

    (A) No, I locked it.
    (B) It needs a new battery.
    (C) Anytime you want.
    (D) A different label.

25. Mark your answer on your answer sheet.

    (A) It begins at 7:30.
    (B) Yes, they're still open.
    (C) They're marked on this map.
    (D) Here, use my key.

26. Mark your answer on your answer sheet.

    (A) Five and two pens.
    (B) It was a gift.
    (C) In the display case.
    (D) At least a couple hours.

GO ON TO THE NEXT PAGE

LISTENING PART 3

Directions: You will hear some short conversations. You will hear and read two questions about each conversation. Each question has four answer choices. Choose the best answer to each question and mark the letter (A), (B), (C), or (D) on your answer sheet.

27. Why was Tod late?

    (A) A schedule was wrong.
    (B) A car broke down.
    (C) Traffic was bad.
    (D) Trains were delayed.

28. Who called the woman?

    (A) A teacher.
    (B) A coworker.
    (C) A salesperson.
    (D) A performer.

29. Where most likely are the speakers?

    (A) At a station.
    (B) At a restaurant.
    (C) At a store.
    (D) At an office.

30. What will the man do next?

    (A) Make a payment.
    (B) Ask a question.
    (C) Deliver an order.
    (D) Leave a building.

31. What is the man excited about?

    (A) A book.
    (B) A business.
    (C) An event.
    (D) An invitation.

32. When will the woman probably arrive at the library?

    (A) At four o'clock.
    (B) At five o'clock.
    (C) At six o'clock.
    (D) At seven o'clock.

List

Akiko Murai — *Marketing*

Josh Bromley — *Accounting*

Eva Stephens — *Administration*

Tim Pritchett — *Research*

Fruit Tree Size Chart

Peach:	5 meters
Cherry:	7 meters
Pear:	9 meters
Apple:	10 meters

33. What did the woman plan to do?

(A) Invite a coworker.
(B) Reserve a room.
(C) Pay a deposit.
(D) Give a speech.

34. Look at the list. In which department does Mr. Howard work?

(A) Marketing.
(B) Accounting.
(C) Administration.
(D) Research.

35. Look at the chart. Which tree will the woman choose?

(A) Peach.
(B) Cherry.
(C) Pear.
(D) Apple.

36. What service does the man offer?

(A) Planting.
(B) Cleaning.
(C) Watering.
(D) Designing.

GO ON TO THE NEXT PAGE

LISTENING PART 4

Directions: You will hear some short talks. You will hear and read two questions about each talk. Each question has four answer choices. Choose the best answer to each question and mark the letter (A), (B), (C), or (D) on your answer sheet.

37. Where are the listeners?

- (A) On a plane.
- (B) On a boat.
- (C) On a train.
- (D) On a bus.

38. What does the speaker tell the listeners?

- (A) Roads are busy.
- (B) Snow is expected.
- (C) Luggage can fall over.
- (D) Some stairs are steep.

39. What does the speaker mention?

- (A) A drink spilled.
- (B) A table cracked.
- (C) A container leaked.
- (D) A window broke.

40. Why is the speaker calling?

- (A) To request a service.
- (B) To explain a decision.
- (C) To assign a task.
- (D) To ask for advice.

41. Where is the museum?

- (A) In front of a gallery.
- (B) Across from a hotel.
- (C) Next to a tower.
- (D) Near a toy store.

42. Why would listeners press 1?

- (A) To reserve tickets.
- (B) To receive directions.
- (C) To leave a message.
- (D) To hear about exhibitions.

43. Who are the listeners?

- (A) Cafeteria workers.
- (B) Music students.
- (C) Theater directors.
- (D) College teachers.

44. What are listeners encouraged to do?

- (A) Review a notice.
- (B) Purchase a ticket.
- (C) Take a break.
- (D) Post a message.

---

45. What is the purpose of the talk?

- (A) To congratulate an employee.
- (B) To explain a schedule.
- (C) To introduce a speaker.
- (D) To present an award.

46. What did Ms. Ramsey do?

- (A) She published a book.
- (B) She traveled overseas.
- (C) She changed her job.
- (D) She studied a plant.

New Technology Talks

Michael Galasso	Virtual Reality
Nina Kallgren	Cyber Security
Norman Turner	Solar Energy
Tina Stowell	Artificial Intelligence

47. Look at the list. Who is the speaker calling?

- (A) Michael Galasso.
- (B) Nina Kallgren.
- (C) Norman Turner.
- (D) Tina Stowell.

48. What does the speaker ask for?

- (A) An address.
- (B) A contract.
- (C) A schedule.
- (D) A catalog.

GO ON TO THE NEXT PAGE

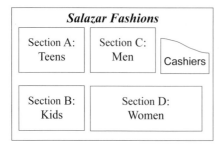

Salazar Fashions

| Section A: Teens | Section C: Men | Cashiers |
| Section B: Kids | Section D: Women | |

49. Why does the speaker thank the listeners?

(A) For submitting some ideas.
(B) For working more hours.
(C) For putting away clothes.
(D) For clearing off shelves.

50. Look at the floor plan. Where will the sweaters go?

(A) Section A.
(B) Section B.
(C) Section C.
(D) Section D.

This is the end of the Listening test. Turn to the Reading test.

READING

This is the Reading test. There are three parts to this test.
You will have 35 minutes to complete the Reading test.

READING PART 1

Directions: You will read some sentences. Each one has a space where a word or phrase is missing. Choose the best answer to complete the sentence. Then mark the letter (A), (B), (C), or (D) on your answer sheet.

Example   Do not _____ on the grass.

(A) find

(B) keep

(C) walk

(D) have

The best answer is (C), so you should mark the letter (C) on your answer sheet.

---

51. Anita has ____ some reports.

(A) preparing

(B) to prepare

(C) prepares

(D) prepare

52. This path ____ to the hotel's pool.

(A) does

(B) leads

(C) starts

(D) takes

53. My travel guide is filled ____ useful information.

(A) for

(B) up

(C) with

(D) from

54. Brennen Styles sells ____ priced business attire.

(A) reason

(B) reasoning

(C) reasonable

(D) reasonably

55. Mr. Davison is the ____ qualified candidate for the job.

(A) already

(B) rather

(C) much

(D) most

GO ON TO THE NEXT PAGE

56. Steve Liu asked that ____ be given a promotion.

   (A) he
   (B) his
   (C) him
   (D) himself

57. Over the ____ few years, Julia Green has studied chimpanzees.

   (A) last
   (B) lasts
   (C) lastly
   (D) lasted

58. The new accountant was late ____ leaving home at six.

   (A) although
   (B) despite
   (C) instead
   (D) even

59. The dishwasher is scheduled to be delivered ____ on Monday.

   (A) clearly
   (B) hardly
   (C) early
   (D) strictly

60. Sam ____ Bill a ride home after school.

   (A) offer
   (B) to offer
   (C) offered
   (D) offering

61. You should decide ____ you are going to wear tomorrow.

   (A) where
   (B) what
   (C) how
   (D) when

62. Because Jane arrived after nine, we are ____ schedule.

   (A) behind
   (B) ahead
   (C) about
   (D) over

63. The vacuum cleaner will keep your carpet ____ and looking fresh.

   (A) clean
   (B) cleans
   (C) cleanly
   (D) cleaned

64. The nurse moved the patient to a ____ room.

   (A) different
   (B) differently
   (C) difference
   (D) differences

65. This running shoe is the lightest ____ on the market.

   (A) that
   (B) one
   (C) any
   (D) each

READING PART 2

Directions: You will read some short texts. Each one has three spaces where a word, phrase,or sentence is missing. For each space,choose the best answer to complete the text. Then mark the letter (A), (B), (C), or (D) on your answer sheet.

Example

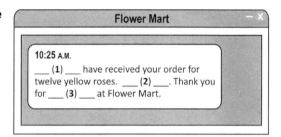

1. (A) We
    (B) Us
    (C) Our
    (D) Ours

2. (A) Please ask for help.
    (B) Red is a bright color.
    (C) They will arrive today.
    (D) Put them on my desk.

3. (A) shop
    (B) shops
    (C) shopped
    (D) shopping

The best answer for question 1 is (A), so you should mark the letter (A) on your answer sheet.

The best answer for question 2 is (C), so you should mark the letter (C) on your answer sheet.

The best answer for question 3 is (D), so you should mark the letter (D) on your answer sheet.

GO ON TO THE NEXT PAGE

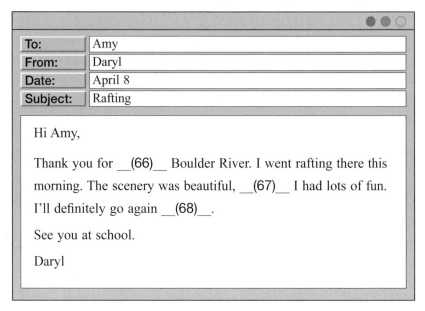

To: Amy
From: Daryl
Date: April 8
Subject: Rafting

Hi Amy,

Thank you for __(66)__ Boulder River. I went rafting there this morning. The scenery was beautiful, __(67)__ I had lots of fun. I'll definitely go again __(68)__.

See you at school.

Daryl

66. (A) recommends
    (B) recommending
    (C) recommended
    (D) recommendation

67. (A) and
    (B) but
    (C) for
    (D) yet

68. (A) somebody
    (B) whenever
    (C) sometime
    (D) everywhere

Questions 69–71 refer to the following notice.

Notice

Your garbage was not picked up __(69)__ it contains glass bottles. These are recyclable. Please separate __(70)__ according to material. The city collects plastic and burnable waste on Tuesdays. Recyclables are __(71)__ on Thursdays. Thank you.

69. (A) due to
    (B) while
    (C) so that
    (D) because

70. (A) trash
    (B) areas
    (C) slices
    (D) outfits

71. (A) collects
    (B) collector
    (C) collected
    (D) collection

GO ON TO THE NEXT PAGE

Questions 72–74 refer to the following text message.

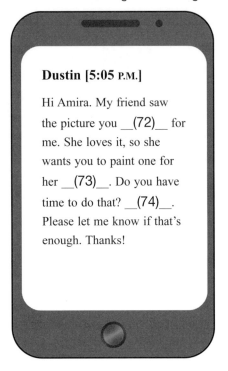

Dustin [5:05 P.M.]

Hi Amira. My friend saw the picture you __(72)__ for me. She loves it, so she wants you to paint one for her __(73)__. Do you have time to do that? __(74)__. Please let me know if that's enough. Thanks!

72. (A) paint
(B) painted
(C) painting
(D) to paint

73. (A) such
(B) too
(C) much
(D) both

74. (A) We're at the art gallery.
(B) The red ones are nice.
(C) I waited for ten minutes.
(D) She'll pay eighty dollars.

Clyde's Coin Laundry

Note that we are not __(75)__ for damage to clothes. __(76)__. If you do, it will not spin properly. In addition, make sure __(77)__ your laundry as soon as the machine finishes. Thank you.

75. (A) productive
    (B) expensive
    (C) responsible
    (D) considerate

76. (A) Extra buttons are on the shelf.
    (B) Thank you for shopping with us.
    (C) Do not put too much in a machine.
    (D) You can exchange bills for coins.

77. (A) to remove
    (B) remove
    (C) removed
    (D) removing

GO ON TO THE NEXT PAGE

To: All managers

__(78)__ Saturn Burger restaurants will soon get a fresh look. We plan to choose six for the renovations. __(79)__. If customers like __(80)__ they look, we will remodel other locations. More details will be provided in February.

Bret McKenzie
Vice President
Saturn Burger

78. (A) Any
(B) Every
(C) Both
(D) Some

79. (A) Each will be in a different city.
(B) We hope you can bring it.
(C) That may be the last place.
(D) A dinner is being held.

80. (A) what
(B) where
(C) which
(D) how

READING PART 3

Directions: You will read some texts such as notices, letters, and instant messages. Each text is followed by two or three questions. Choose the best answer to each question and mark the letter (A), (B), (C), or (D) on your answer sheet.

Example

Milltown Supermarket

We have the freshest fruit and vegetables in town!

Opening Hours
Monday to Friday, 9:00 A.M. to 9:00 P.M.
Saturday and Sunday, 10:00 A.M. to 7:00 P.M.

1. What does the store sell?

(A) Food
(B) Clothing
(C) Books
(D) Furniture

2. What time does the store close on Tuesday?

(A) At 7:00 P.M.
(B) At 8:00 P.M.
(C) At 9:00 P.M.
(D) At 10:00 P.M.

The best answer for question 1 is (A), so you should mark the letter (A) on your answer sheet.

The best answer for question 2 is (C), so you should mark the letter (C) on your answer sheet.

GO ON TO THE NEXT PAGE

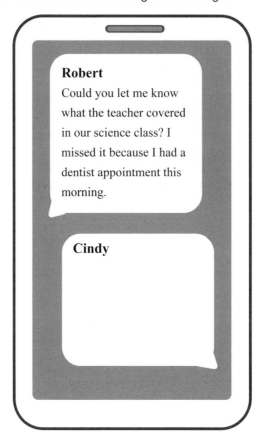

Robert
Could you let me know what the teacher covered in our science class? I missed it because I had a dentist appointment this morning.

Cindy

81. What does Robert ask Cindy to do?

(A) Call him in the morning
(B) Tell him about a lesson
(C) Make an appointment
(D) Teach a science class

82. Select the best response to Robert's message.

(A) "It's already covered."
(B) "OK, I'll inform them."
(C) "I'll give you my notes."
(D) "Until last night."

Questions 83–84 refer to the following notice.

Attention

Skyarc Airline's flight 471 to London has been delayed due to bad weather. The departure is now scheduled for tomorrow at 8:40 A.M. Passengers can receive vouchers at the Skyarc ticket counter for meals and an overnight hotel stay.

83. Where most likely is the notice?

(A) At an airport
(B) At a hotel
(C) At a bus station
(D) At a restaurant

84. Why should people go to a counter?

(A) To request a refund
(B) To make reservations
(C) To choose a meal
(D) To get vouchers

GO ON TO THE NEXT PAGE

Questions 85–86 refer to the following information.

Contest Rules

Entries for the Costume Design Contest must be submitted by October 18. Please do not send the costume itself. Instead, provide us with front and back photos. We will also require a written description of your entry. It should include the materials and accessories you used to make it. For more details, visit www.arcfashions.com.

85. According to the information, what must be sent?

(A) One drawing
(B) Two pictures
(C) An entry form
(D) A costume

86. Why should people visit the Web site?

(A) To find contest information
(B) To read about fashions
(C) To order accessories
(D) To watch an award show

Janet
I just heard that the starting time of our afternoon match will be 1:45. And we'll be playing on Court A instead of Court D. The organizers moved our game because lots of people will be watching us. The one that we'll be playing on has more seats around it.

Pauline
OK, thanks. I'm having lunch with volleyball players from another team now. You should come.

Janet

87. What does Janet say has changed?

(A) A time
(B) A restaurant
(C) A team
(D) A location

88. Select the best response to Pauline's message.

(A) "It usually does, I think."
(B) "I've had something already."
(C) "I believe it took an hour."
(D) "Yes, it was delicious."

GO ON TO THE NEXT PAGE

TEST 1

TEST 2

TEST 3

REEVE's DINER
The Best Burgers in Town

We're open every day from 11 A.M. to 11 P.M.

Weekday Specials
Regular burger.. $7.80
Cheeseburger $8.50
Double burger.. $9.90

Weekend Specials
Chicken burger $8.50
Bacon burger $9.20

These special prices include fries and a beverage.

Try our new shrimp burger, which we are offering at all our locations until the end of August!

---

89. What is NOT offered at a special price on Fridays?

(A) The regular burger
(B) The cheeseburger
(C) The double burger
(D) The bacon burger

90. What is included with the specials?

(A) A dessert
(B) A drink
(C) A coupon
(D) A toy

91. What is suggested about the business?

(A) It sometimes closes earlier.
(B) It sells hotdogs.
(C) It has several shops.
(D) It serves shrimp burgers all year.

Questions 92–94 refer to the following online chat discussion.

 Wendy's Messages

Nathan [3:56 P.M.]
Wendy, the sandwiches for Watkins Advertising are ready. Are you still out making a delivery?

Wendy [3:57 P.M.]
Patrick is driving. After our delivery, he went down the wrong street, and he didn't know where we were. But we're on our way back now.

Nathan [3:58 P.M.]
Good! I'll need help loading the food into the van. After that, you'll have to leave immediately.

Wendy [3:59 P.M.]
Don't worry, Nathan. Watkins isn't far, and we have until five to get there.

92. Where do the writers probably work?

(A) At a moving company
(B) At an advertising agency
(C) At a catering company
(D) At a car rental agency

93. What problem does Wendy tell Nathan?

(A) An order was canceled.
(B) An address was wrong.
(C) An employee was late.
(D) A driver got lost.

94. What will happen at around five o'clock?

(A) A party
(B) A delivery
(C) A repair
(D) A presentation

GO ON TO THE NEXT PAGE

Questions 95–97 refer to the following article.

Come Out to Applaud the Dolphins

Myersville (Oct. 17) — The Myersville Dolphins won the County Cup on Saturday. To celebrate, there will be a parade on October 28. It will start at Town Square and end at Tilbury College, exactly where the team practices. The school's coaches, cheerleaders, and a marching band will join the event too. Some of them will hand out team caps to fans.

City mayor Riana Vernon made the announcement today. "Our city's top football team has never won the trophy before," she said. "I hope lots of locals come out to show them how delighted we are!"

95. Where will the parade most likely end?

(A) On a shopping street
(B) On a public beach
(C) On a sports field
(D) On an outdoor stage

96. What will some people receive on October 28?

(A) A trophy
(B) A ticket
(C) A hat
(D) A shirt

97 What does Ms. Vernon hope people will do?

(A) Watch a football game
(B) Read an article
(C) Show the trophy
(D) Attend the parade

To:	Miguel
From:	Tammy
Date:	May 9
Subject:	One Suggestion

Dear Miguel,

I had so much fun living with you and your family last month. Your relatives are all nice, and your house is beautiful. Portugal is amazing, and you showed me some great places.

You mentioned that you wanted to study English in England next summer. Yesterday, I picked up a brochure from a place south of London. Students there enjoy camping while learning English. Since you enjoy doing both, I think you'd love it. I'll send that to you in the mail.

Write me some time to let me know your plans.

Your friend,

Tammy

98. What does Tammy say about Miguel's family?

(A) She lived with them.
(B) She sent them a parcel.
(C) They booked a tour for her.
(D) They are visiting England.

99. What is suggested about Miguel?

(A) He sometimes goes camping.
(B) He recently moved to London.
(C) He works for a travel agency.
(D) He is a hotel manager.

100. What is Tammy giving Miguel?

(A) A painting
(B) A video of a class
(C) A brochure
(D) A school list

Stop! This is the end of the Reading test. If you finish before time is called, you may go back to Reading Parts 1, 2 and 3 and check your work.

マークシートは切り離してご利用ください。

または専用 Web サイトで A4 用紙に印刷できる PDF データを配布しています。

ダウンロードして、そちらをご利用いただくこともできます。

採点は、便宜的に 1 問 1 点に正解数をかけて計算してください。

専用 Web サイト

https://www.ask-books.com/978-4-86639-396-4/

第1回テスト

Score ／100

Date ／　／

〈切り取り線〉

LISTENING TEST

Part1 No.	ANSWER A B C D	Part2 No.	ANSWER A B C D	Part3 No.	ANSWER A B C D	Part4 No.	ANSWER A B C D
1	Ⓐ Ⓑ Ⓒ Ⓓ	11	Ⓐ Ⓑ Ⓒ Ⓓ	21	Ⓐ Ⓑ Ⓒ Ⓓ	41	Ⓐ Ⓑ Ⓒ Ⓓ
2	Ⓐ Ⓑ Ⓒ Ⓓ	12	Ⓐ Ⓑ Ⓒ Ⓓ	22	Ⓐ Ⓑ Ⓒ Ⓓ	42	Ⓐ Ⓑ Ⓒ Ⓓ
3	Ⓐ Ⓑ Ⓒ Ⓓ	13	Ⓐ Ⓑ Ⓒ Ⓓ	23	Ⓐ Ⓑ Ⓒ Ⓓ	43	Ⓐ Ⓑ Ⓒ Ⓓ
4	Ⓐ Ⓑ Ⓒ Ⓓ	14	Ⓐ Ⓑ Ⓒ Ⓓ	24	Ⓐ Ⓑ Ⓒ Ⓓ	44	Ⓐ Ⓑ Ⓒ Ⓓ
5	Ⓐ Ⓑ Ⓒ Ⓓ	15	Ⓐ Ⓑ Ⓒ Ⓓ	25	Ⓐ Ⓑ Ⓒ Ⓓ	45	Ⓐ Ⓑ Ⓒ Ⓓ
6	Ⓐ Ⓑ Ⓒ Ⓓ	16	Ⓐ Ⓑ Ⓒ Ⓓ	26	Ⓐ Ⓑ Ⓒ Ⓓ	46	Ⓐ Ⓑ Ⓒ Ⓓ
7	Ⓐ Ⓑ Ⓒ Ⓓ	17	Ⓐ Ⓑ Ⓒ Ⓓ	27	Ⓐ Ⓑ Ⓒ Ⓓ	47	Ⓐ Ⓑ Ⓒ Ⓓ
8	Ⓐ Ⓑ Ⓒ Ⓓ	18	Ⓐ Ⓑ Ⓒ Ⓓ	28	Ⓐ Ⓑ Ⓒ Ⓓ	48	Ⓐ Ⓑ Ⓒ Ⓓ
9	Ⓐ Ⓑ Ⓒ Ⓓ	19	Ⓐ Ⓑ Ⓒ Ⓓ	29	Ⓐ Ⓑ Ⓒ Ⓓ	49	Ⓐ Ⓑ Ⓒ Ⓓ
10	Ⓐ Ⓑ Ⓒ Ⓓ	20	Ⓐ Ⓑ Ⓒ Ⓓ	30	Ⓐ Ⓑ Ⓒ Ⓓ	50	Ⓐ Ⓑ Ⓒ Ⓓ
				31	Ⓐ Ⓑ Ⓒ Ⓓ		
				32	Ⓐ Ⓑ Ⓒ Ⓓ		
				33	Ⓐ Ⓑ Ⓒ Ⓓ		
				34	Ⓐ Ⓑ Ⓒ Ⓓ		
				35	Ⓐ Ⓑ Ⓒ Ⓓ		
				36	Ⓐ Ⓑ Ⓒ Ⓓ		
				37	Ⓐ Ⓑ Ⓒ Ⓓ		
				38	Ⓐ Ⓑ Ⓒ Ⓓ		
				39	Ⓐ Ⓑ Ⓒ Ⓓ		
				40	Ⓐ Ⓑ Ⓒ Ⓓ		

READING TEST

Part1 No.	ANSWER A B C D	Part2 No.	ANSWER A B C D	Part3 No.	ANSWER A B C D
51	Ⓐ Ⓑ Ⓒ Ⓓ	71	Ⓐ Ⓑ Ⓒ Ⓓ	91	Ⓐ Ⓑ Ⓒ Ⓓ
52	Ⓐ Ⓑ Ⓒ Ⓓ	72	Ⓐ Ⓑ Ⓒ Ⓓ	92	Ⓐ Ⓑ Ⓒ Ⓓ
53	Ⓐ Ⓑ Ⓒ Ⓓ	73	Ⓐ Ⓑ Ⓒ Ⓓ	93	Ⓐ Ⓑ Ⓒ Ⓓ
54	Ⓐ Ⓑ Ⓒ Ⓓ	74	Ⓐ Ⓑ Ⓒ Ⓓ	94	Ⓐ Ⓑ Ⓒ Ⓓ
55	Ⓐ Ⓑ Ⓒ Ⓓ	75	Ⓐ Ⓑ Ⓒ Ⓓ	95	Ⓐ Ⓑ Ⓒ Ⓓ
56	Ⓐ Ⓑ Ⓒ Ⓓ	76	Ⓐ Ⓑ Ⓒ Ⓓ	96	Ⓐ Ⓑ Ⓒ Ⓓ
57	Ⓐ Ⓑ Ⓒ Ⓓ	77	Ⓐ Ⓑ Ⓒ Ⓓ	97	Ⓐ Ⓑ Ⓒ Ⓓ
58	Ⓐ Ⓑ Ⓒ Ⓓ	78	Ⓐ Ⓑ Ⓒ Ⓓ	98	Ⓐ Ⓑ Ⓒ Ⓓ
59	Ⓐ Ⓑ Ⓒ Ⓓ	79	Ⓐ Ⓑ Ⓒ Ⓓ	99	Ⓐ Ⓑ Ⓒ Ⓓ
60	Ⓐ Ⓑ Ⓒ Ⓓ	80	Ⓐ Ⓑ Ⓒ Ⓓ	100	Ⓐ Ⓑ Ⓒ Ⓓ
61	Ⓐ Ⓑ Ⓒ Ⓓ	81	Ⓐ Ⓑ Ⓒ Ⓓ		
62	Ⓐ Ⓑ Ⓒ Ⓓ	82	Ⓐ Ⓑ Ⓒ Ⓓ		
63	Ⓐ Ⓑ Ⓒ Ⓓ	83	Ⓐ Ⓑ Ⓒ Ⓓ		
64	Ⓐ Ⓑ Ⓒ Ⓓ	84	Ⓐ Ⓑ Ⓒ Ⓓ		
65	Ⓐ Ⓑ Ⓒ Ⓓ	85	Ⓐ Ⓑ Ⓒ Ⓓ		
66	Ⓐ Ⓑ Ⓒ Ⓓ	86	Ⓐ Ⓑ Ⓒ Ⓓ		
67	Ⓐ Ⓑ Ⓒ Ⓓ	87	Ⓐ Ⓑ Ⓒ Ⓓ		
68	Ⓐ Ⓑ Ⓒ Ⓓ	88	Ⓐ Ⓑ Ⓒ Ⓓ		
69	Ⓐ Ⓑ Ⓒ Ⓓ	89	Ⓐ Ⓑ Ⓒ Ⓓ		
70	Ⓐ Ⓑ Ⓒ Ⓓ	90	Ⓐ Ⓑ Ⓒ Ⓓ		

マークシートは切り離してご利用ください。

または専用 Web サイトで A4 用紙に印刷できる PDF データを配布しています。

ダウンロードして、そちらをご利用いただくこともできます。

採点は、便宜的に 1 問 1 点に正解数をかけて計算してください。

専用 Web サイト

https://www.ask-books.com/978-4-86639-396-4/

〈切り取り線〉

第2回テスト

Score

/100

Date   /   /

LISTENING TEST

Part1			Part2			Part3			Part4		
No.	ANSWER		No.	ANSWER		No.	ANSWER		No.	ANSWER	
	A B C D			A B C D			A B C D			A B C D	
1	A B C D		11	A B C D		21	A B C D		31	A B C D	
2	A B C D		12	A B C D		22	A B C D		32	A B C D	
3	A B C D		13	A B C D		23	A B C D		33	A B C D	
4	A B C D		14	A B C D		24	A B C D		34	A B C D	
5	A B C D		15	A B C D		25	A B C D		35	A B C D	
6	A B C D		16	A B C D		26	A B C D		36	A B C D	
7	A B C D		17	A B C D		27	A B C D		37	A B C D	
8	A B C D		18	A B C D		28	A B C D		38	A B C D	
9	A B C D		19	A B C D		29	A B C D		39	A B C D	
10	A B C D		20	A B C D		30	A B C D		40	A B C D	

Part4		
No.	ANSWER	
	A B C D	
41	A B C D	
42	A B C D	
43	A B C D	
44	A B C D	
45	A B C D	
46	A B C D	
47	A B C D	
48	A B C D	
49	A B C D	
50	A B C D	

READING TEST

Part1			Part2			Part3		
No.	ANSWER		No.	ANSWER		No.	ANSWER	
	A B C D			A B C D			A B C D	
51	A B C D		71	A B C D		91	A B C D	
52	A B C D		72	A B C D		92	A B C D	
53	A B C D		73	A B C D		93	A B C D	
54	A B C D		74	A B C D		94	A B C D	
55	A B C D		75	A B C D		95	A B C D	
56	A B C D		76	A B C D		96	A B C D	
57	A B C D		77	A B C D		97	A B C D	
58	A B C D		78	A B C D		98	A B C D	
59	A B C D		79	A B C D		99	A B C D	
60	A B C D		80	A B C D		100	A B C D	

Part1			Part2		
No.	ANSWER		No.	ANSWER	
	A B C D			A B C D	
61	A B C D		81	A B C D	
62	A B C D		82	A B C D	
63	A B C D		83	A B C D	
64	A B C D		84	A B C D	
65	A B C D		85	A B C D	
66	A B C D		86	A B C D	
67	A B C D		87	A B C D	
68	A B C D		88	A B C D	
69	A B C D		89	A B C D	
70	A B C D		90	A B C D	

マークシートは切り離してご利用ください。
または専用 Web サイトで A4 用紙に印刷できる PDF データを配布しています。
ダウンロードして、そちらをご利用いただくこともできます。
採点は、便宜的に 1 問 1 点に正解数をかけて計算してください。

専用 Web サイト

https://www.ask-books.com/978-4-86639-396-4/

第3回テスト

Score　／100

Date　　／　／

〈切り取り線〉

LISTENING TEST

Part1 No.	ANSWER A B C D	Part2 No.	ANSWER A B C D	Part2 No.	ANSWER A B C D	Part3 No.	ANSWER A B C D	Part4 No.	ANSWER A B C D
1	A B C D	11	A B C D	21	A B C D	31	A B C D	41	A B C D
2	A B C D	12	A B C D	22	A B C D	32	A B C D	42	A B C D
3	A B C D	13	A B C D	23	A B C D	33	A B C D	43	A B C D
4	A B C D	14	A B C D	24	A B C D	34	A B C D	44	A B C D
5	A B C D	15	A B C D	25	A B C D	35	A B C D	45	A B C D
6	A B C D	16	A B C D	26	A B C D	36	A B C D	46	A B C D
7	A B C D	17	A B C D	27	A B C D	37	A B C D	47	A B C D
8	A B C D	18	A B C D	28	A B C D	38	A B C D	48	A B C D
9	A B C D	19	A B C D	29	A B C D	39	A B C D	49	A B C D
10	A B C D	20	A B C D	30	A B C D	40	A B C D	50	A B C D

READING TEST

Part1 No.	ANSWER A B C D	Part1 No.	ANSWER A B C D	Part2 No.	ANSWER A B C D	Part3 No.	ANSWER A B C D	Part3 No.	ANSWER A B C D
51	A B C D	61	A B C D	71	A B C D	81	A B C D	91	A B C D
52	A B C D	62	A B C D	72	A B C D	82	A B C D	92	A B C D
53	A B C D	63	A B C D	73	A B C D	83	A B C D	93	A B C D
54	A B C D	64	A B C D	74	A B C D	84	A B C D	94	A B C D
55	A B C D	65	A B C D	75	A B C D	85	A B C D	95	A B C D
56	A B C D	66	A B C D	76	A B C D	86	A B C D	96	A B C D
57	A B C D	67	A B C D	77	A B C D	87	A B C D	97	A B C D
58	A B C D	68	A B C D	78	A B C D	88	A B C D	98	A B C D
59	A B C D	69	A B C D	79	A B C D	89	A B C D	99	A B C D
60	A B C D	70	A B C D	80	A B C D	90	A B C D	100	A B C D

マークシートは切り離してご利用ください。
または、専用 Web サイトで、A4 用紙に印刷できる PDF データを配布しています。
ダウンロードして、そちらをご利用いただくこともできます。
採点は、便宜的に 1 問 1 点に正解数をかけて計算してください。

専用 Web サイト
https://www.ask-books.com/978-4-86639-396-4/

●著者紹介

鈴木 瑛子（すずき ようこ）　LISTENING PART3,4 READING PART3 解説担当

東京海洋大学 特任准教授。ジョンズホプキンス大学大学院修了、コミュニケーション学修士（M.A.）。著書に『TOEFL iBT® テスト 必修フレーズ 100』（ テイエス企画 ）、『論理的に話す・書くための英語変換術』（三修社 ）、共著に『TOEFL ITP® テスト完全制覇』（ ジャパンタイムズ ）などがある。英検 1 級、TOEIC® L&R 990 点（満点）、TOEIC Bridge® L&R 100 点（満点）取得。

渡邉 淳（わたなべ あつし）　LISTENING PART1,2 READING PART1,2 解説担当

フリーランスの編集者・ライターをしながら、東京海洋大学で非常勤講師を務める。著書に『TOEIC® L&R TEST 戦略特急スコア育成計画』（ 朝日新聞出版 ）など。英検 1 級、TOEIC® L&R 990 点（満点）取得。

X: @nabe_atsu3

はじめての TOEIC BRIDGE® L&R テスト 完全模試 3 回分

2021 年 6 月 25 日　初版　第 1 刷
2025 年 1 月 15 日　　　　第 4 刷

著者............................鈴木 瑛子／渡邉 淳

英文作成.....................Daniel Warriner

発行者........................天谷 修身

発行　　　　　　株式会社アスク
　　　　　　　　〒 162-8558
　　　　　　　　東京都新宿区下宮比町 2-6
　　　　　　　　TEL：03-3267-6864
　　　　　　　　FAX：03-3267-6867
　　　　　　　　URL：https://ask-books.com/

装幀............................岡崎 裕樹

印刷・製本.................株式会社ディグ

ISBN 978-4-86639-396-4　　　　　　　　　　　　Printed in Japan

乱丁、落丁の場合はお取り替えいたします。
弊社カスタマーサービス（ E メール：support@ask-digital.co.jp）までご相談ください。